When the Body
is a Guardrail

poems by

Kara Dorris

Finishing Line Press
Georgetown, Kentucky

When the Body is a Guardrail

Publisher: Leah Maines

Editor: Christen Kincaid

Cover Art: Brett Thompson

Author Photo: Charles Head

Cover Design: Brett Thompson

Order online: www.finishinglinepress.com
            also available on amazon.com

Author inquiries and mail orders:
Finishing Line Press
P. O. Box 1626
Georgetown, Kentucky 40324
U. S. A.

Table of Contents

*A guardrail is, first & foremost, a safety barrier
intended to shield a motorist who has left the roadway,
& should be installed when consequences of striking a
guardrail would be less severe than striking other
objects nearby.*

~ The Federal Highway Administration

I used to be Snow White, but I drifted.

~ Mae West

*We, afflicted by ourselves,
gladly afflicting, gladly
needing to be afflicted.
We, who sleep with our anger
laid beside us like a knife.*

~ Rainier Maria Rilke

One

Say You Say

Say you stare at the highway
as if it were the way to keep your madness
at bay. A way to know there is always a *to*
& *from, a here* & *there* like a letter
or keepsake always finding new ways
of interpretation. Say you say the highway
is really a river & the cars are as rudderless
as leaves. Say you say the early morning
light you drive into is not the same
evening light you drive out of, that yellow
median lines blur like memory. Say you say
each song the radio offers to the wind
was—once upon a time—you, &, somehow,
still is.

Disappeared, TX

She fell into containment
the way women & tropical birds fall.
A recent escapee of Tupelo, she nursed soldiers
in DC & skinny-dipped waterless on rooftops.

What did she know of MP uniforms
or the men beneath?
That cages come in so much flesh & breath?
Then she fell into fairy tale:

a fatherless husband, a mother, & seven
brothers-in-law. Sold gas & sundries
at the Dorsey General Store,
learned we construct cages out of open spaces.

Sold the loneliness of a dirt road,
the company of dog packs & cigarettes—
trust me, she'd say, *you learn to romanticize the past.*
But there is no Dorsey anymore,

only a suspension bridge over Ripley Creek,
a small Texas town swallowed by another.
She remembers the way that store held
hostages, how water inside

the water tank felt like metal in the sun.
You say, she should've run away. But where to?
Small towns are all the same
to the disappeared.

Highway Elegy

Like truck drivers feel highway
beneath foundations & home
beneath vanishing roads, we miss
the Red Riding Hood of midwest
fairy tales who wears cowboy boots
& rawhide gloves, her crimson feet
mirroring raw hands.

We build towns along highways
& name them, even if
we pass in a blink & never know.
In between, we leave chunks
of memory, fuel, & bile in ditches
when our temperatures rise too fast
from one hour to the next.

So, we drive. Texas, Louisiana, Oklahoma—
Arizona, New Mexico, Texas.
The telephone lines tighten. Or maybe
we project our skin on anything
that stretches further than it wants to,
that feels out of date in our stomachs.

Perhaps the lines resent not only
the weight of birds
or intimate calls without faces,
but the design of following highways
like lovers who don't want to be led.

With each mile marker, touchless
connections feel more real, all lonely shiver
                              & hot breath.

My Texas Hansel & Gretel

Somewhere between the cowboy church & a biker
fellowship on Highway 4 lives a family. We wake
to the rev & spit of Harleys, the sputtering yum
of diesel & snakes in gas tanks. We sleep to hooves
& heels & 4 wheels. Eat breakfast bullets
fired by the gun maker, our neighbor,
Mr. Bond Arms—we enjoy the way he welds us
so easily into Kevlar skins, like potato sacks
& animal peels. He employs my brother & I to find
stray shells & frags, breadcrumbs. With a metal
detector, we flag the scatter pattern & collect
motorcycles & men decorating the highway.
We collage our mailboxes with *what is left
behind*. Living against the highway has taught us
how to hit debris at the sweet spot so it flies up
& at the car behind—the balm of speeding 120
miles an hour, speed that keeps us
from saying what we mean. When we anger,
we name it *indigestion* & buy all the Pepto
Bismol. We like the way the pink tastes of internal
organs, bright & frilly against the steel & asphalt spoon.

Sign with Child's Head Missing

Look. You will see family, seemingly
on their way to the drive-in
riding in a rusted car so square,
at the beginning, now deceptively
curved. Clear license plate—tiny L & A,

something of loss & annunciation,
headlights as big as caves
as if one upon a time we needed more
light to announce ourselves,
& maybe we did, when stars

were brighter than cities, streets less lit
with neon. See the parents smiling
at the bundle of headless delight
that is their child—a father's slick,
dark head, a mother's pinned waves—

the child senses the beginning—the bleeding,
the wars—comes to face it without
a face, without a mouth
or eyes, nothing to invent sense with.
See the manor house behind

shuddered in trash & framed in ruin
framing the family, the rips
in the canvas like birds, no, like
the escape routes of birds that must
have burst from the child's head.

Look closer you see the rips
are actually silhouettes of mustangs
& the cowboys who break them,
& you realize your mind didn't lie,
not entirely, that breaking spirits
& the need to do so always
creates gaping holes.

Country Life is Like the Negative Side

of a film strip, nights of small survivals
& small sacrifices bleeding through until
you can't tell one from the other.

Until guessing at ghosts is the only thing
left. I know, I hear the moans,
giving birth to litters on the air, I hear

the coyotes taking what they think
is theirs. I hear the protest, the mediation
between mother & nature: take
this one,
                        not those two.

Prayer for Winter

Each morning, we tend pecan orchards
& trim our table in bread.
As if our hands are baskets, we reach

& pull, bend & lift, filling & filling
until we can't anymore.
You have seen it, I know, you

who must know the texture & weight
of everything & hate it.
We feel less like ourselves when we harvest,

less like our skins are soaked dresses
& more like you. Like you, we steal
from scavengers who mistake

themselves for the sum of the world.
It's an innocent crime, you might say,
a power play, a shadow, an omen.

This is when the white buffalo,
dressed in snow drifts, calls our names,
choking on wind & distance. Only you know

if, or when, we will meet.
You know we try.
Each day we go out, bend & lift until

our weaved hands are full.
But are we only duty's bit & whip?
Where is the release, when we will know

everything is possible
& suddenly nothing is necessary?
Tell us we are more

than pack animals broken long ago,
carrying satchels of splinters & hollow pecans,
who only disbelieve in rescue & relief.

Landscape with Cowboy Church

You expect belief—when corralled you think
handlers force submission—

but beyond Jung & horse whisperers, who knows
dreams, the wild
tangerine half-heart of the kept?

What is worth more: humans or the things we ruin?

Our family classifies as a cowboy church:
a rodeo arena & a red-scraped barn,
enough barbed wire to corral a herd of mustangs—

at least, enough to bind each set of hands folded
in each square foot   of each four acres
                   listed on the deed deeded to us.

We own an underground well, a right, & pay
in collection plates.

Guns enough to protect what's ours.

We keep the cattle tank full, easy access for heads
& hands to fall into.

Elegy for the River that Was

Can we still call it a riverbed
when it's infested only with moss & dew, tadpoles
& the baby jumpers they grow into?

We feel our way with our eyes,
not the soles of our feet, we slog only through
the heaviness of heat—

10 feet tall & 10 feet wide, water rushes beneath
the highways in pipes, beneath the hooves
& muzzles of livestock, bales of hay.

Water rushes from a manmade lake into a natural one,
into the betrayed side of the dammed riverbed,
the life of the never-should-have-been

exchanged for the dying.
Water stolen to cool the nearby nuclear plant.
Don't worry, my second dad says,

the reactor isn't as big as it seems.
The 10 story walls, 13 feet thick, are just for containment.
Can we call it reassurance & mean illusion?

Who knew water could act like a pack of snakes,
embed itself as easily in absence as presence—
that stone mimicked the flow of water,

could take water's place when dammed—
as we walk the dry riverbed, tiny frogs jump
away from our feet. We must seem 10 stories tall.

Why We Named the Oceans

I wanted to call you today—you who thinks the physical is everything—
to share an 18th century philosophy: *every world is a word to conjure with.*
What is the world but the words we used to conjure it into meaning? How we
remake country & county lines, redefine maps based on geopolitics, patriotism,
tectonic plates. We named the oceans so we knew where we sailed, so others
could know, could follow. How even you are an architect of your own language.
I thought, how can you not hear what I'm hearing? If you could see words as
levers & thermostats, parts of heating & cooling units, as clean air & proper
maintenance or as decay, as hair & dust clogging a filter. What I take away is:
see both sides & be careful: you can't undo harm. Consider the dimensions of
space-time—height, width, depth—so many elements to factor in. & although
words are worldbuilders, to admit such power would be to name the way you
bully & shame, always insisting, always, that you are a good man. But really
Novalis wrote, *every word is a word to conjure with. Whichever spirit calls—
another such appears.*

Like Snow

We live on the highway for a fast getaway.
Skunks, armadillos, & others small animals are hit
& thrown into our gravel drive,
we shovel the dead bodies like snow.

I guess we shouldn't leave out the hay & oats
or watch from warm, fog windows as
raccoons have babies or stags
teach does to blend into darkness.

We should dismantle our halogen
bulbs & outlaw Christmas lights.
Use car horns as lights, as footsteps,
open the windows & stick out hands & heads,
wave downwind. But we don't.
Instead we hunt with our everyday accessories:
just like our neighbors.

One day a car hit a buck & ran, threw
that warm, lost fawn body into our driveway,
an offering. My second dad went out with a knife
& sawed the antlers off. He said, *here, a bridegroom.*

As Delicate as the Skin Over a Girl's Wrist

I grew up reaping, he says, *cutting the pulse,*
separating the seeds at harvest.
You have a choice. It must be terrible, he laughs,
to only do what you want.
Sometimes it is. He doesn't ask how.

We keep penicillin in the fridge, needle
in hand, for horses with open-sore eyes
& listlessness. He thinks penicillin cures our wounds—
but the impossibility of our want cuts us,
deepening lines across wrists.

Is he bleeding out from this cut,
this desire to be here & anywhere else? Between
who he is right now & who he wants to be?

I want to spill through the field every day,
collect flies, burrs, & snakes. I want
to raze it, drive the tractor & till the earth,
be buried, post-bloom, beneath.
I want to stand with those two forgotten horses
& flood their isolation with my own.

Instead, he tells me if I need something to do
I should clean the filter on my AC unit,
toothpick a blade of grass,
or harvest the wings of something smaller,
then thrash it. But I don't amputate—
I hold on, saturate winged veins
with the salt & sweat of my fingertips.
So heavy this stain, beetles never fly again.

My second dad doesn't understand why I don't kill—
he will shoot a goat to stop its suffering,
amputate his finger to stop infection,
then use this loss to scoop peanut butter from the jar.
He can't grasp the small deaths,
the self he sacrifices as executioner.

Yesterday, he unknowingly slit his palm
fixing a thermostat, then wiped sweat
from the wing of his forehead, left a trail of blood.
Today, Freon burns bombard his knuckles.
My stomach tightens as I imagine
his skin healing, microscopically bridging
a distance his wide hands can never measure.

His hands that only sing to mechanical things.
When the body is merely a hammer,
what have we ever consciously mended
that was more heart than machine?

He will fight against anything,
scratch at the wounds as he works.
About suffering they were never wrong;
we drive on. The thorn tear on his forearm,
the bubbled bee sting on my cheek,
when I thought, *you are not good enough,*
when he said *we aren't a family.*
We never apologize.

We like to make Kool-Aid pickles,
sour to pineapple or lime to sweet,
turn what is into what it never wanted to be.

We have places to go. We sing to Patsy Cline
& take the asphalt road away from itself.

Briar Rose Crash-Tested

Once there was a girl who seized
at loud noises—her brain heard *danger,*
an overly sensitive duck & cover,
donned a putty-pink safety helmet.
When she walked, she held another's
hands tight, afraid to take
the earth from itself. She glowed alien,
a metal-plated girl, birdcaged
between human tuning forks.
What chance did her heart have against
its own beating? The knocking
of her knees? Fireworks, horns,
& slamming doors, trains, bombs, & blue
whales? *Boom*, down. You remember
thinking: her children will inherit
an easy way to torture their mother,
how easily they will be tortured.

With Guns Drawn

Of the many virtues, hope is the one you nearly forgot
—Melissa Kwasny

When a limping old man tried to film under your skin you saw him, not his intentions, not his angled hand against his angled hip, angling your way. Did your knee-high boots, palm tree dress in winter represent a fantasy? a memory? a fairy tale? The world, desperately dangerous, so do what you love & damn the consequence, a Bluebeard collecting women anyway he can. Your lover almost decked him, said, *he'd probably done this before,* but you only saw how empty his story's moral must be. Are the blue veins beneath your skin hieroglyphics? Did he want to wander your deep, decipher pictographs, remember what he'd lost before he knew to remember. He walked reverently. *Probably doesn't even limp,* your lover said. You didn't consent. Did he want to uncover the spiritual glow of your bones? He isn't the first man who tried to steal your soul. That old man on the Paris subway, knobby hand on your knobby knee, weaponized with grandkid pictures. It's no small thing to hope for the best. What if you had been a female gunslinger double-fisting Rugers, if you hadn't been pink & oblivious, at the end of whatever youth remains?

From Wolves

She went missing for two days, between
the slamming back door & the hanging.
When she left, barefoot & blue-sweatered, wintered
in anger, he thought *she can't get far*—

he shouldn't have slapped her face,
should've listened when she said *a dolphin's
fins resemble our limbs*—
her transformation took two days.

Winter sleet fused her fingers & feet,
fused sleek arms to thighs, hands that once spun
braids the wind twined into noose,
thread & bark shredded as her body swung,

threads of her father's sweater, the one
he wore when he hung himself ten years before.
She remembered the day;
she had asked if dolphins evolved from wolves

& her dad had answered, *yes, little cub,
we did.*

Elegy for a Snow Day that Did Not Belong to Her

Imagine your second dad as a boy in the snow—
15 inches, he says, *in Texas.*

You try to imagine yourself waist-deep
& hungry, but you can't.

It is not your memory,
the way Syrinx was never Pan's,

but a story told by a distant man,
the way wind speaks through river reeds.

Those reeds, your father's hands
as he swears 15 years later, he & his first family

survived 15 inches of snow again.
We didn't have heat, we almost died, he says.

That year, snow camouflaged the rural highway,
left only the top inch of the barbed fence.

No one dared the highway until
an egg delivery truck ditched itself. *A loss,*

the driver said. *A loss. Take everything—*
so they did. Father & his other daughter.

They bundled eggs in shirts & hats,
in pockets of pants, filled coats of eggs,

& wheelbarrows of eggs.
You try to imagine your father

pushing you in that red wheelbarrow—
beside, beneath, above so much breakable flesh—

but you can't. The breakable thing touching you
has always been your own skin.

On that day, they threw egg snowballs
unafraid of breaking.

They tongued yolk popsicles
& smacked lips covered in yolk chapstick.

Frostbit & shivering, even the deer's mouths
& hooves turned into eggs.

Your father reached for his shotgun but the shells
were eggs; he fired anyway.

The deer's eyes colossal as eggs.
That night, your father fisted egg whiskey cups

as a family swore yolk blood oaths
to always stay the same.

It was that kind of day,
a day that encouraged you to promise everything.

That year, the snow took everything—
the doorless barn, the ravine, the hopscotch board

belonging to that other daughter.
Nothing else could be salvaged but instinct.

Safe in your second father's arms,
that other daughter navigated a new world

when accident reclaimed survival—
imagine, a snowed-invisible highway

& a ditched egg truck might have saved a family—
temporarily, when swearing to stay meant

you were honor-bound to leave—
but we can't speak of accident without speaking of birth—

It happened to your father & his other daughter.
It did not snow in Texas today.

When the Body is a Guardrail

The snow cannot hide
disappointment over the idle
& the dead. & it's true
we too have nothing to offer
but a soft-wet emptiness
snow already understands.
We let our ditches
become washed-out bridges.
Our road-kill, trophy mirages.
Let gold meridians
& guardrails disintegrate
into breadcrumbs & suggestion.
We mountain weightlessness
into weight, lone into loneliness.
We learn to pull on flak jackets
& silence gracefully
without gracing our skin.
We learn to tread with stealth.
Earrings jangle
like an aftermath of traps.
But still, the snow cannot forgive us
easy captives, fat depressives
lost in surrender. We cannot
forgive each other.
Snow days remind us why
we long to drive into a volcano
or drive-in movie
to forget our weight makes
its own ghost in snow.
We simply cannot give
each other what we need.
It's not that we don't know how
but that we refuse
to be someone we are not,
the other refuses too.

Two

We do not describe the world we see.
We see the world we can describe.
~ Rene Descartes

My Highway of Sure Things

[…] every day, past a barn
like an aquatic mural,
rainbow trout or diseased goldfish.
I call it survival art like the rings
of trees, like graffiti, but really it's rust,
the just getting by of time, second-hand
smoke lungs. Did you know
a goldfish's hunger is permanently
set to obesity? We love to watch
as they instinct themselves
to death […]

∞

[…] yesterday, we found lizards
behind our house doing it again.
An offense to justice honoring
a hydrangea bush I killed with
a happy love. On the back porch
in plastic, hunter-green containers,
sit open-mouth replacements full of
Miracle Grow & shame. For
the ground's sake, for the sad goldfish
we buried dressed in toxic bedazzle
beads & memory, I wanted to wait
a full year to announce recovery,
to absorb the French fry bits & salt
& blackberry seeds I used to kill Fish.
But the lizards only have eyes
for each other & don't believe in stories
with tragic heroes or closing actions […]

∞

[…] we did a revision exercise Thursday
naming all the body fluids we could
think of & writing stories.
We shared tales of dismembered
limbs & pimps. Everyone
laughed & gagged & I thought
what's so gross about boogers & snot
& semen & blood? *Haven't they ever
dug up a dead goldfish or been in love before* […]

∞

[…] in a circle drinking—
women gulp strawberry beeritas
& men drink Shiner Bach.
A guy in a white shirt says
you need a frame-by-frame heart.
The women nod,
think hummingbird hearts
can't be captured by camera hearts.
We listen for waves, but humidity
is as close to wet as we get.
It tells us: white shirt guy hit
one of us, but no one remembers who.
We all laugh as if waiting
for a fist-full of moon […]

∞

[…] in red
heels & toenails, let
sparrows on stakes direct us:
transmogrification this way.
We have a choice beyond flight:
wolf-dress, armadillo,
or porcupine […]

∞

[…] our stomachs should
be more than gas & air
the size of a football field—
that definition best fits
the lungs when the heart says
break. But the filmy stomach
has no roof to break
itself against—it can either
negotiate with ego or relent to
falling & vertigo […]

∞

[...] always spot the ceiling,
keep your eyes open—
witch hazel, ammonia, consumption tonics—
for the last time, every time,
we memorize the screen door's view,
our hands against piano—
man/beast antiseptics, virgin oil extracts—
the plaster constellation of ceiling
spins faster—
corn remedies with Jamaica ginger, hemorrhoid cream—
each prescription
sounds the same failed rhetoric
of our bodies [...]

∞

[...] in the black void of the monitor's
sleep mode, I see flashes of
vengeance across the screen
like flashes of pain
across my brother's face.
I see *'Vengeance,'* not *'Vergence,'*
not only because my mind searches
the void for a real word,
or because we are trapped
between verge & converging—
I am hunting truth in a morphine drip
that has my brother saying *I let them
hurt him*, but fear I am just
another patient, less patient
with another's pain [...]

∞

[…] as if my hands are just another fence
to scratch an itch against
our donkey rubs her flank, her face
against my palms, another chain-linked border
the way fingers spread both to catch & slip through
the moment, the apple, the heavy layer
of dirt coating her mane,
linking skin to memory, to both sides
of story when story is the way I see
& the way you don't […]

∞

[…] dads wander streets inside—
we never knew how many ways
to be homeless
existed within the body.
Without street signs like Vena
Cava or Glucose Row,
how can he know my body
when I don't? Which finger
is he camped in? Is he sleeping
beneath the overpasses
of my wrists? If legs
are highways, are feet & hands
states? Or countries patrolled
by muscle & blood vessels?
Breasts are endless
fields. My eyes stretch & fog,
offer hunters' blinds as solace
for solitary shadows […]

∞

[…] life in 3D—
dandelion puffs as flashlight beams
through trees, light beneath freckles,
freckles erupting like the five stages of grief:
the leaking ends—we are meant to
leak out, we want it to end—putty, play-do,
pudding, & wood glue can act the dam
against a river leaking—*leaking, leaking,*
leaking—I guess we'll keep on
leaking, I guess we kinda like it […]

∞

[…] immigrant sand not grass,
but this is no Dover Beach,
no *ignorant armies clashing at night*
except for us who live within
the city limits. Our manmade beach
lines Pearl Street, traps
us in ourselves like a bikini.
If the city council only knew the menace
the sea brings—hairspray, pacing,
ransom. The beach is congested
on cold & flu days when
no one remembers to swim.
We become threats to passing cars
& life preservers, to 911 operators
& cell towers […]

∞

[…] two fathers each two loves—
I wish I could say one was the sea,
swelling tide against a buoy,
breath of air between deep dives,
endless, interchangeable open of sky & water.

I wish I could say one was a daughter,
fingernails of collected coral shells,
anatomy lessons like lesions,
lungs drawn in sand labeled *heart*.

I wish I could say one was love itself,
another word for sea or daughter
& the connective tissue of highways between,
but all I see are two narcotics: duty
& its opposite, oblivion […]

∞

[…] *don't be afraid of the suffering*, she said, *our ghosts
are ghosts of our own choosing* […]

∞

[…] what radio stations do we tune ourselves
to for dialogue or hush?
Our antenna hands receive static
the way clothes cling to skin
& spark when pulled from a dryer.
We shake free but absorb electricity
like sweat between lovers holding hands,
when one pulls away the other follows—
we forget our projector faces aren't
simply drive-in theaters we can choose
to leave when the credits begin […]

∞

[…] when carving out land & providing
for family, the Ditch-Witch
needs a Bobcat. When we play *Left 4 Dead,*
my brother kills any zombies in my path.
Someday we'll turn into swiftly moving air
that doesn't give a damn
about the faces we used to have […]

∞

[...] in 100 degree weather I can't forget
sweat, the killing, panting heat,
the release of artificially cooled air
& then I miss home, my second dad
telling stories about crawling through attics
to fix AC units, the burn of
insulation in the scrapes
on his arms & hands, scrapes more
a part of him now than I am. His hands,
so much more beautiful than mine,
more choice & necessity, the pus & calluses,
the pads so used, so trained,
so forced into hurt [...]

∞

[...] always paint yourself reaching,
eyes on that rich fist, curled & grasping
fingers on the verge of ripping
canvas, ripping myth, nails broken
& knuckles blooded. The choice is this:
looking down at your hands working
or up at your hands imagining the work's
possibility [...]

∞

[…] it's easy to efface ourselves,
to be supplicants to the everyday mortars,
head down to task, lost in it
& the background until textures of
our skin & task merge into one
endlessly hot, gritty desert afternoon
with buzzards circling lower
& lower to pick at what is left,
one scavenger recognizing another […]

∞

[…] so many turtle girls
at the circus, living in tiny
water-filled boxes,
these bodies, how difficult
to pierce the surface,
the pointing fingers,
the laughter, our shelled backs,
our self-portraits.
Beneath the showman's
words the world only sees
itself […]

∞

[…] we want
like the breath of air
between deep dives, dissect desires
like anatomy lessons […]

∞

[…] driving home, 30 motorcycles stop traffic
& run red lights, helmetless,
as if it's okay to risk everything—
what about that girl night-driving
home without headlights?
Does she know she takes her family
with her, anyone who stays & stakes
a claim. That she never really loves
because she always wants to be someone
different, & if she is not who she is
right now, they cannot possibly belong
to their present selves either […]

∞

[…] *look for umbras—to be in the shadow*
of anything is to be safe.
Survivor knows the price
of safety; once she had been one
of seven. Donkeys are bred to protect
smaller animals, but the last,
a male, shook two others
to the neck-death. Coyotes got
the rest. But now, with a new protector,
Survivor has her favorite blade
of grace, cold & smooth grass,
a pet frog named Farce. Can run
into the pecan orchard as if into
a field full of mothers, bury
her apricot-mouth in someone's
hands […]

∞

[…] stripes breakup the body's line
to fool predators.
The bars between us—
you & me, white tigers & lemurs—
who do the stripes protect?
At the gorilla cage,
watching lovers on display
I drop my camera. It echoes.
A lover runs away.
His big, flat face wondering
where she went. I did that.
Red-drift roses, his eyes.
My eyes rest against
a flamingo's infinity neck […]

∞

[…] lightning crowds the house,
metal dinosaurs of abandoned ancestry—
we burned TVs first, then wall-
crosses, open gun safes, & gloves.
We can't sleep in the nightlight
of our mother's voice saying
waking is the hardest thing to do.
When we say, *wake up anyway.*
We're like a German circus family
collecting peregrines,
in a wild west shootout for tent space.
Last one standing wins […]

∞

[…] so still—her body reflects
the steel hibiscus of her mind.
She still calls me by her mother's name,
steals something every time.
Her hands in diabetic dark aren't still,
they worry, they steal […]

∞

[…] we survive. Survivor winters,
knees to ground, hobbles for sun,
sees us so far away—
she understands we prepare letting
go before we let go, thereby letting go
before the let thing is gone.
We anticipate our loss, deny
the bullet between her eyes.
Her front hooves don't feel
rot or field or tongue,
but her back hooves work fine,
& with ass in the air,
she pushes her face against rocks,
knows her face feels like apricot
to stone […]

∞

[…] living in a Texas flood plain,
we think water is a natural right.
Because we own it, we need
flood insurance. Because we own it,
when clouds open & call our bluff,
we stand it out, rehearse
the fallout […]

∞

[…] ducklings hatched
in our sometimes pond,
& Survivor's face was their first.
She loved like a mother,
but they died, of course,
you knew that. Sometimes,
what is   is your only option—
A few weeks later, raccoons
crossed highway: three babies
smashed. We watched
their carcasses fester into
road for a week. A mile down,
the mother, stomach up, teats-full
& side-heavy. Survivor scraped
what she could in the dead
hours, knew she was a family's
last chance to feel like apricots
in someone's mouth […]

∞

[…] baby ladybugs look like ticks
until we lean in & see red so small
we think it can't be ours. Our blood
feels like everything, like pavement
is bread, bed, & love to ticks
rolling along, falling into the usual traps:
cracks, grass, handprints in fresh
concrete. We knew we'd kill
& still […]

∞

[…] vertigo is when you think you know
what something means,
but don't.
& you can't
____(blank)____the same
as everyone else.
My grandfather took me tailgating
in his blue & white Ford,
home to braided
air-conditioner parts & ladders,
skinny arms & legs.
My feet scraped road as he navigated
the best neighborhood hills
to fly up & down […]

∞

[...] we inherited this land,
drafted into it without inspection,
an heirloom—
What else to call it?
The way it is or
a bad real estate investment [...]

∞

[...] *because it wasn't beautiful, but it was*
ours, & it was all we had [...]

∞

[...] we excavate memories the way
we excavate ancient civilizations, sifting
through the layers of a day's, a week's,
a millennium's dust-bunnies.
A decade feels like a thousand years
trying to retell our origin stories,
peering through the glare of kaleidoscopes
& glass lids, sieving the dust
of prejudice & ruin, digging through
the dead skin of compromise & desire [...]

∞

[…] we're human, we cover
the decay—hand out pig snout
as chew toys,
accelerate into tailspins,
repurpose anger-tossed rocks
as mosaics & fine china […]

∞

[…] my second dad is blinded to the rainbows
Rainex makes on windshields
in the carwash,
as if the glass is a ball pit
at a playground
meant for light or the eye
like when you spend your time
looking at the distant
through a kaleidoscope,
instead of running towards
the nearest an exit.
Only one of us sees beauty & terror
in the reaction of separation,
in not letting water drown itself
in itself but slide divided
into the metal drain beneath us […]

∞

[…] we reach for anything with
a coppered shine—
at hospitals, nurses say *check
your hands at the door.*
My grandfather filled a glass car
with pennies. I've tried
& failed to chart sense,
to timeline the last 30 years
in cents. Time is funny that way,
beholden only to itself.
In 30 years we've never changed
the battery of the fleur de lis
clock always ticking away
like highway guard markers […]

∞

[…] act fast: finches steal,
mistake fingernails for pennies—
act fast: someone will
trade pennies for quarters—
you have to act fast:
one minute you're there & the next […]

∞

[…] imagine humidity has edges,
that each drop is unique—
or is that us? These arms, earrings of bone,
drench my shoulders—
we like to think each sin,
each ounce of sweat we expend,
each way we sin is ours—
the only way to rid the body
of this arrogance is to race across
flooded bridges & fly down hills,
all dangles & limbs, as fast
as we can […]

∞

[…] the night sky is suckerpunched,
laid flat by lightening,
the dark tunnel of back
country roads is dissected & given
horizon. We are suckerpunched
by the day, wish we could take it back,
want to suckerpunch tomorrow,
offer candles & alchemy
to the blind, name roses
tell-tale hearts. Say *when, enough,*
know the difference between
goosebumps & razor rash,
the difference between the dark
we're heading into
& the dark we've left […]

∞

[…] as her tumor dragged,
we treated Survivor with apples
& absence even as it hindered
her from retrieving
the so-called treat of our hands.
We've never known when to
administer that needle
of oblivion; instead a small-caliber
gun to the head so she dies
slowly waiting for the rifle.
Pain is pain, dead is dead
my second dad says. Yet he believes
the bluebonnets lining Texas highways
are more beautiful when
mixed with red Indian paintbrushes,
a gathering of wildness.
The way he defines degrees
of beauty proves he feels
beyond the machine of his hands […]

∞

[…] he says
his mother's death
proved the world only
makes sense
if you force it to.
I know he is right
because want is force,
& we want more
than anything
& we make the world […]

∞

[…] hoarders of small things:
pennies & sand castles,
the glue, snot, & tears or whatever
moistness binds molecules.
Rapunzel, her braided brains
a set of reigns, hanging out
the window. We believe in escape
tunnels & salvation, in oceans
we hear inside shells,
& even oceans we haven't found
yet […]

∞

[…] the difference between driving lost
& looking is an artist's signature,
a blood-spattered *trying*,
the bright pink of a fresh highlighter
studying *how* not *why* […]

∞

[…] for a breath between I-35
& home, the stomach believed the eye—
the bridge blinked & nothing but sky
& the unknown-to-be-filled-in
defined us. & that's all we remember,
a wormhole & a woman steering
the Chevy ahead, her bright pink elbow
out the window trying to capture
air, the nothing rushing, the cup
of her palm so inefficient […]

∞

[…] scorched in Texas unevenness,
we forget we don't own gravity, even soaking
wet & then that last wave bites you
on the ass, an aquatic *I told you so.*
We forget as humidity hangs in the air,
as moisture soaks skin in the fairy tale
of ownership. We won't admit our want
to let gravity own us, to let the sun
& moon determine when we sleep.
Underwater we become colossus & less
than 100 pounds, a perfect size for everyone […]

∞

[…] but, please, don't forget
1.   how much death-mass weighs in goldfish
2.   that instinct is a calorie we never shed
3.   lizards are allowed, even encouraged, to do it behind
        hydrangea bushes
4.   it's okay to bloody yourself for love
5.   ride highways like tides
6.   dream of being sailboats
7.   sometimes spinning is a good thing
8.   & sometimes not
9.   but always, always, always find an object to spot […]

∞

Three

Elliptic Orbit

Are you a sun or planet?
If you are a planet, what is your sun, *that autonomous
ever-luminous* star your body attunes itself to—
money, love, beauty, truth?

Or are you a sun? & only you
can make yourself run? Do others attune
themselves to your needs? Can you generate
a magnetic field, misread the word & turn
into a fiend, shoot solar winds

to force the long-gone back? Did you know
the sun makes up 99.8% of the solar system's mass?
Can you fill so much space?
Are you your own calculator
of day & night, competition to the moon?

Is your moon the unconscious? If dreams are asteroids,
can you maintain the orbit of three trillion
comets & icy bodies? The sun holds such weight—
but did you know billions exist
throughout the Milky Way, that you

sustain you, but to everyone else, you're only
one more ball of glowing gas?
Can you see the way radioactive x-rays devour
the atmosphere, &, still, somehow, color
like rainbows? Can you look away?

A Thousand Lives Lived

We circle gently, aisle by aisle tracing objects
with heated fingers, plunder fabricated dining rooms,
closets, & libraries—your hands linger on romantic pins,

costume rhinestones sewn into bracelets & earrings.
We amble past the splintered & inked printer's tray
spooning the painting of a moose

spooning the river. The river leads
us towards vintage dresses, all lace & moth holes,
to ladies' hats like bird nests. You pause before

the painting of two horses along a fence line,
gray & roan, watery in watercolors.
You want to offer, palm-up, some version of comfort.

We worry; these objects don't merely exist for us to take.
They have histories, scratches, chips, & marker initials.
A person existed somewhere for every object,

a person exists: elephant music box, bottle ceiling light,
Grand Canyon postcards, stained glass windows,
pink elephant drink stirrers, & comet door knobs.

The glass unicorn with crisscross wings
& wedded legs, the one your mother gave you,
is a member of a glass animal zoo.

You pass, aisle by aisle, & imagine a thousand rotations,
a thousand lives, maybe even a thousand versions of your own,
each life changed by each item bought, items warmed

by the hands of others: U.S.S Arizona in a bottle,
Scarlet O'Hara plate, Waterford crystal—
each sits on your mantle.

Item by item, you imagine yourself into history, incalculable memories. You may never know what ghosts you've rehomed.

Another Eden

Every beloved object is the center of a paradise
—Novalis

We leave Eden & never know,
always searching for the lost
before we knew to lose it.
It seems only fitting
each action is a loss of something—
we shuffled out
of bed this morning, even leaving
leaves: sleep, to awake,
to dressed, to the day gone by.
When did we decide
paradise was all or nothing,
when did we realize
seduction is a form of disappointment?
We live in paradises of moments,
until the moments are gone,
as if momentary gestures are everything,
as if Eden is only made up of flesh
& things, the flesh & things
changing with our desires. Who said
memories can't sustain us?
If what they say is true,
that love is a wound, it is enough
that the body fits inside
whenever it needs to.

Under the Missing & Innumerable Stars

He might be homeless, but you know where he lives—
exposed to the streets & fists, moon & mosquitoes,
the red & blue pulses married to police sirens.

At 3 a.m. his home is a post-tragedy parking lot,
as hushed & hollow as your bedroom.
Beneath lids, the white of your eyes flicker like headlights.

You wound, prick & scab your arms like your own mosquito,
sweat & nails, bit & sting. The sound
of sheets dragging across each other, across skin

is as close as you get to hearing sirens.
Intimacy is knowing where someone sleeps.
You shadow his trail of paper-bag bottles.

His starved body, his hands never crusading & never crafting,
as feral as your father's. The presence of those fevered,
black-tinged fingers is why you retreat,

but his eyes are a bronzed balm, not a toxic hazel,
& this absence is why you remain.
Intimacy is projecting your memories onto others.

Your father could be homeless somewhere too,
a victim of cocaine or foreclosure. He could be
sleeping in an alley between 7/11 & someone else's patio,

or dead or alone. But you know: Intimacy is
wondering if someone you love is dead or alive,
loving someone for simply who they are not.

When you sleep flush against hands that accept you;
when you are born into hands that do not.

Atlantis

The simplest words contain the most, I know,
& I know simplicity is about consolation.

I know we *goodbye* to define
watching what we love disappear like sunlight

into night sky. That we goodbye to make
a leaving permanent, I know, because knowing

what you've lost is lost forever is a healing
balm. I know language is always strategic & intimate,

learning to bear what seems unbearable,
&, perhaps, I know we delude ourselves into

believing coping means drowning loss deep.
The end means *never*, the end means *release*,

I know, the end means *vagrancy*, the end means
remember, please, because this comet will never

covet our orbit again. The end is a moment
of preparation & sirens, I know, the end is a moment

to etch against forgetting, to allow yourself
to forget, I know all this, & yet—

Elegy for Stone Sisters Sunk in a Father's Stomach

You want to be the kind of daughter
who throws egg snowballs
& builds yolk forts for cover.
Who tests gravity by mouthing eggs
then skating on frozen lakes.
But when it snows you know blood slows,
the sun angers when it cannot incite
water to boil. When it snows you know
the moon is mirrored everywhere
& more cruel.

Your second dad is not a man of regret,
but on snow days you worry he grieves
those other daughters never born,
the ones who never regret.
You mourn the river that once flowed over
the stone snake paths, snow-covered
tree fossils no one climbed except
to feel something collapse.

Those other daughters are safe—
from indecisive hearts & slow-firing neurons
damming the body's rivers. From boys
who kiss & dim, novels that ruin, vodka
that spins the room into an abuser's direction.
From the light of dead stars that remind us
not everything seen is alive, not everything alive,
seen.

Still House, Hollow Lake

Everyone sieves—but when what fills is nuclear
waste, invasive algae, when

you are nothing but a manmade lake
populated just for

human lures, a sport made hallow by waiting,
flicks of our wrists & baiting,

you should be afraid—somedays
I believe I will always be a still house

on a hollow lake. Like the day I drove to Austin
in the rain, passed a sign I swear read,

Elegy Highway, a toll road, & it made sense
that we must pay with grief's coin

for loving & wanting & needing & driving
lonely roads. I couldn't pull over, I couldn't stop—

not for food or fuel—just kept
misreading the exit ramps, over & over again,

until there were no exits left.

A Study in Light

We are filled by a backward yearning for the dark.

Black paint dominates Francis Bacon's self-portrait,
reflects face like a mirror—did the artist know
we would, *like in everything else,*
see ourselves?

The way our first dad
took us to friends' houses, Toys R Us,
but never home. Did he know kids shouldn't wander
shadowy rooms of an addict's brain?

Was he afraid we would read ourselves in the black
of menthol & meth? I want to say each created a halo or exit sign,
to find beauty or reason,
but a poet once said *we can't always be poems about light.*

In Phillip Guston's painting "Light" gray haze
shrouds black squares, showing
not all light illuminates beyond itself.

In "Wharf" light glows from beneath,
dampened by sea & blood in the water,
by the brackish buildings & cliffs like heads to get lost in,

& somehow, I am the wound & bruise in the middle,
submissive to the dominatrix of longing
when longing is, as another poet said, *three parts burnt salt.*

The Secret Lives of Railroad Crossings

Desire protects nothing but itself—
how many bodies have bedded down with metal rails,
awaited vibration, whistles of speed?
You only hear about the ones who choose
not to leave &, in doing so, leave forever. The ones
who camouflage themselves, find order through a pinhole
of lightning pain, striping the rest of us
of tethers.

So heavy, these bodies as beams, finger splinters,
as they carry us without ever moving &,
in doing so, move more than we ever will,
at least, in the ways that matter, & so
matter not at all as the world vibrates us apart,
replacing us with new beams.

But you find clarity on these rails, the fear,
the possibility of drifting, &, in doing so, drift forever
on some slow country road, one you can lay across & never
see another living soul, & so,
see all the souls who have drifted before.

Everyone Knows Moonshine Tastes Better Illegal

Texas law states when two trains meet at a railroad crossing
both must stop & neither can leave until the other is gone—

a dad screams at a mom for asking about insulation,
a mom yells at a dad for opening her UPS package.

Sitting at Braum's, he says *that bitch,*
for the first time, she said she hated me last night,
& he sounds surprised.

He plays hard, hard-to-get, but it's just hardness
to get under your skin
& you refuse this childish need childishly.

He calls pain *sight*, just another physical sensation
that begins & ends—

& you love this luxury of tough, this learned craving
to know only what you can erase,
to be Corpus Christi, a disappearing beach.

You ask him, *is this your (logically private) pleasure?*
You wonder has pleasure been replaced with idleness?

He says, he can't leave, he can't stay—he is always losing.

He says, *best to be neutral*   *but if you can't*
it is better to be pissed off   *than pissed on.*

Off & on he says with the DNA of his body, his hands steady
around the French fry bits & plastic ketchup container,

& you don't know how to tell him,   *you've tried,*
god, you've tried & never
managed one without   *the other.*

By Any Other Name

You read *crackhouse* in the sidewalk cracks,
in the zigzag patterns of ants,

crackhouse in the police cars cruising,
in the cockroach cups

& ghostly plastic bags blown across yellowed grass.
Crackhouse in the wrecked windows,

in the stenciled skulls over peace signs.
Your brother says tagging has been traced to

the Roman Empire, preserved by
the eruption of Vesuvius. It seems

we have always had the urge to declare
& curse ourselves, to scratch our names

beneath bleachers, in the DNA of our children,
in the cities of our dead. But is it enough

to substitute a name for our presence?
In what letter, what curve or line lies

your brother's search, stepping over twisted
tourniquets & arms as thin as needles,

finding your dad so high in a crackhouse
he didn't recognize his son? We step over

so many bodies navigating those we love—
it has been a harsh winter. The coyotes devoured a nest

of raccoons, & you learned you cannot afford to love
things that are not fenced. Do all these bodies

make up the *o* in your last name? Is the final *r*
your reaching arms or your father's?

What do we know about the names we are given?
We know the holes in the boundaries,

to sacrifice the out of bounds glyph over the *i*
like a firebug caught in the glow of undressed lightbulbs.

We know to walk through the *dorr* of Dorris to be alone.
We wait. But searching is a kind of waiting;

it's the divide between being better as a daughter
& being better as *his* daughter.

Your brother has always been the better son of everyone.
When he walks up to a crackhouse he ignores

the tagging that reads *addicts only*. No one stops him.
I guess there is an addict in us all.

Past the Gates of Acme Forge

Your brother drove you through the past today, your dad's house, truck wheels turning onto Lebo St. You remember to forget the route, this learned forgetting lets you get lost even driving home. Hand steady at the wheel, your brother looks for a black '67 Camaro, a legacy promised but sold a decade ago. All that is left is the knowledge that old muscle cars & fathers jackrabbit easily, fall away from your hands. Your brother taught you how to drive with a one-handed carelessness, a gangster slouch, & a need for speed, an inherited stance. *Dad saved my life once in a car crash*, he swears. Maybe that's why your brother takes offerings of cigarettes & beer. You played at the gates of the Acme Forge, imagine your dad getting high between metal pipes & acrid, hot forges at night. You don't want your brother to know you would never recognize your dad's house on your own. What you do remember is distant—sitting in your dad's lap. He has taken something, a ring of keys, a lighter, an action figure. At first, it's a game of keep-away, but when you try to steal it one last time, he gets angry. You learned showing needs equals shame. But today your brother drives by just to see if your father is alive, as if the house could spill secrets. You focus on the present: your brother's breath is smoke-filled & easy. Your fingers trace your lace dress. You want him to brake or drive so fast houses bleed together, you want your dad to be sitting outside sober. But your dad isn't home today. You don't know if you feel let down or let go. What is left, you call his landmarks— ruptured driveway, drying shrubs. The lines of neglect, like the lines of cocaine across a mirror, like the lines of your father's face reflecting not love, but need, & the absence that comes swiftly before & after.

Coming Back was Like

coming out of carbonite
it would take a scrolling screen at the start of Star Wars
       to explain

like re-walking gravity after a lightyear in space

like being night but   day-dressed

like a pitch-black night after the Luminale Festival

like remembering gothic architecture pre-airstrike
       or heating an ice-covered hotel

like embracing the shield between riot & riot police
       or training a falcon as a pelican

You were a long time away, coming back was like
       forever carrying the child you used to be
         in the suitcase of your elbow

A Second Encounter with a Little Princess

As if tea leaves in a cup, I stare at a potted plant & read the sign beneath: lemon balm surrounded by milk & honey lilies. From behind, I hear a prim voice asking, *can you be more specific, please?* I turn to see a miniature Snow White complete with the blue & white striped hoop skirt & buttercup corset. Her mother laughs, *Okay. Turn the bottle upside down, squeeze gently, a little into your palm, penny-sized. Then rub the sunblock on your arms where the sun can see.* Staring at the little fairy tale, I see freckled skin beneath cap sleeves. Her long dark hair pulled haphazardly from a face intent on measuring. Did my mother look at me that way? You are with me now; your brown hair, trails from my scalp, but we cannot claim Snow White—our horses & princes have cantered away. I wander past a Chaste Tree. My first kiss was in secret, slouched in the backseat of his parents' Lincoln. Only after driving past the street to my house three times, did I finally breathe. Did you see it on my face? Another first, in the bed of his white truck. Did your mother know about your firsts? Under an Afghan Pine, Summer Snowflakes wrap cement bench legs, warming my calves. Did your mother play loose with you? No, she forced you still on deck loungers for portraits; your lounger was my fireplace ledge, & you wondered why I always cried in photographs. Your mother sewed my own dress in razzle-red velvet with a full skirt like those women wore in old American westerns; lace trimmed layers. I posed at the fireplace, carefully arranging ruffles. Still, we both cater & barter as taught, save the "good" clothes for later. Today—not picture perfect—your stillness, this bench holds no heat, my ripped jeans & your torn shirt are not lacy or delicate.

Supernatural Scrabble

Like an *I love you* written over a newspaper
obituary, she loves the husband of
another widow. I've never understood holding
another's hand or the scrabble of gravestones.

I've only grasped those who turn away,
the ones who screw in those metal letters
for money, so heavy, even in pictures,
your coffee table collapses, so heavy miners
could be trapped under, but breathing keeps them
like breathing keeps me awake at night,
when I feel his breath & recite
Grimm's fairy tales where breathing derails
everyone into danger.

My grandfather didn't warn her, that Mississippi
girl, about Texas burrs until she sat
among them one day screaming, until he carried
her into the house laughing, *now you won't forget.*
She shouldn't have expected anything less
from a husband who built windmills.

She won't tell us his name,
but now my grandmother loves a man
she can't have but tells me I'm going to hell
for living with one. She wanted to name me
Melissa so I'd be *Mel* or *melting.* Perhaps she knows
something I don't. You need to keep
names secret, small gods, so no one can call you
to places where you don't belong.

Like Shiva

Getting a mani-pedi is something like getting embalmed—
soak skin & nails in heated tonic,
expose the soft underneath.
It is not unlike the womb, I think,

this return to water before
returning to separate atoms of matter.
Polish & place hands inside molten candlewax bags.
Wax cools, cements your hands.

I know we harden before we cave.
This is Sunday. For seven days I will perform
seven tasks my grandmother feared—
paint her nails neon pink & cut

her hair pixie short—
until I only regret what's done.
It's quiet today, & I'm quiet in my grief
but not without contact—

my body my house, I choose silence,
closed heart as wax encases my hands & feet,
cringe against buffing
that strokes away the evidence

of my living & grief.
We've been brought low, humors rushing out
& pooling like tides without satellites—
you can fail someone by forgiving too easily—

I will dream every night of another
granddaughter posing in water, facing brine
& pockets of rocks, wearing a lace dress
some other grandmother sewed,

another kid's Micro-Machines & mermaids
drowned in the flowerbed.
I don't want to know this new family;
I want the places & people I leave to stop existing,

especially that house, already on its way into history
through decades of stillness & staring—
but I'm afraid we will forever know best
those who leave.

Who are we in heaven? Our best reflection?
Is she a young mother, a widow,
a bitch, an Atlantis?

An Afternoon of History

Watching junkies dumpster-dive for food
& half-smoked cigarettes,
Christmas Eves, my brother parks
at the 7-11 downtown & doles out Reds.
Something about his stillness attracts the loneliest.

Some years our first dad never shows.

All I can imagine is Twain's spoonful of water
dripping since Troy fell, since the pyramids
& foundations of Rome were new,
since Christ was crucified & Columbus sailed,
5000 years falling, & not enough
for one human's insect need,
that spoonful of water dripping now, still, & forever

when all this is just an *afternoon of history.*

Prayer for Comfort

Why did my brother have to find
our father transformed

by junk, more plant than man,
a state where pain's absence teaches nothing?

Did you create pain as a figment
of the human mind?

My brother said, *I have cancer.*
You watched as our father said, *yes,*

I know, it's in your mother's bones.
We invent countless ways to comfort,

to extend the pain threshold.
I know knowing we can carry

more pain than we think is a comfort.
Take me to this moment quicker,

to the edge of tide & sand, grit
& flood of injury. I want to know

what you know, for us to hold signs
that say *point to your shoreline of pain*

& I'll point to mine. Then anyone
could hurt us, we could hurt anyone

as easily as you. Then we would understand
why rose thorns are a kind of mercy,

why our hands are a kind of thorns,
why you save wisteria from wanderlust

& saved the dusky seaside sparrow
from itself. You have shown us

that we are all creatures of the day,
rememberer & remembered alike,

that we are some sense of the seed
we emerge from, of the seeds

that emerge from us. You have shown us
the moment we know we should stop

searching, but don't—when the warmth
of a falling star is a death wish,

the escort of a funeral motorcade,
when steps forward are steps into

catacombs, & the weight of our sky
is the weight of the sea.

Elegy for the Last Iron Bridge, Rainbow TX

The AR-15 will be light in my arms, spring action will save my shoulder from recoil, but nothing, *nothing*, not even distance, will save my target, a zombie bulls-eye at 1,000 yards. Inside rifle's tiny scope, the eye changes between red & green, so I know precisely where hurt will hit—but we get to Uncle Merle's too early, & it's closed. So, we drive. Down the strip of highway housing Dairy Queen & Chevron, past produce market & fields of hay. Stop at Sonic, drink highways inside Styrofoam cups. My brother shows a picture of our first dad's new house, a tarp tented over the bed of a long dead pickup truck. Every homeless man is a reminder of where we come from. So we drive. Over an iron bridge, & when I say, *go under again, I want a new picture*, my brother laughs & u-turns as gravel spits beneath tires & light shutters.

The Deer Stand

Once a girl & a boy collected pecans in a land
not their own. They wanted to be place—
the place time wants to be, a tangible *found.*
Turned eyes to sky, saw vultures dive
for anodyne (that *found* thing that gives away self):

a second dad thought he found himself in AC & heating repair,
metal wrench & snapping leather belt;
a mom & brother found depression, giving
tree & yellow whiffle bat; a first dad only absence;
a daughter, seafoam etched letters, & her bridegroom's
antlers perched with seagulls.

& then they found family—in the pink & grey
deer stand, swollen like a cow that swallowed strawberries
& Pepto—an array of rifles & scopes,
a pile of fieldstripped firearms
& unlocked safeties.

Living as Flood Plains

is not easy, no places to hide, no insurance for high risk lands. It means our hearts are rain-flooded during storms, flooded with home & guilt & *now what* when skies clear. So, we are always flooded by what stands aboveground, by what seeps beneath, & yes, we need it to live, but it needs us to drown, to be filled past brim, which means whatever we plant washes away, only wildflowers survive day to day. You say, *did I not remember to warn you that it could never be Eden?* But which one? Eden of Perfect Innocence, Eden of Deer & Wolf, Eden of Being & Body, Eden of Memory, Eden of Home & Away Again. You're right: bombs & tantrums don't forgive, & we are nothing but bombs & tantrums. Yet, sometimes, can't we choose to be balms of light & wonder?

What the River Says

So, you were never empty, were you?
Never without
the distance of unseen
consequence, the way river
never quits prophesying, at least,
to those of us who live on rafts,
who bait our feet
over dock's edge any season.

We hunt it, hunt alongside it,
trimming its sides with our threaded
traps, know all good survivalists
stick close, cleanse hands
in water that cleansed the stag.
So, what if river drowned you once,
once it buoyed you, teaching life as regret,
so much so you regretted yourself right

into another life. You worry
when your river freezes
it might never recover, but, I argue,
even the rivers of Texas summers survive,
leak themselves further, faster, deeper
become magnets
for the poles of our bodies
inviting dragonflies & skin, always

whispering, even when
the grass is taller than the tallest
Texas tidal wave, when the hottest sun
forces water to find shelter within
the earth's darkest, still whispering when
undercurrents become an ascent,
an exit.

Folding 1,000 Cranes (A Wish)

When road appears wet, your accelerator foot
instinctively lifts, chest sways, leans

into expected spin
even as you know we live in

a drought year, that dew's dictatorship
has not saturated this far,

you have already slowed, been passed
by another car. Drive after drive,

you commit the same act & expect
something different, but this instinct feels

like mistake, like the mirage is not
the wet glistening on pavement

but the belief that you can teach instincts
to behave. You want to believe

the shimmer can be more than danger or absence—
a thousand abandoned wings

in the swirling shitstorm of routine.
You forget that wonder can be found even in

what something is not
or not   even pretending to be.

Acknowledgments

"My Texas Hansel & Gretel" appeared in the *Fairy Tale Review*

"Sign with Child's Head Missing" and "Like Shiva" appeared in *Without Words: An Anthology of Silence. Kind of a Hurricane Press*, 2018

"The Secret Lives of Railroad Crossings" appeared in *Wraparound South*

"As Delicate as the Skin Over a Girl's Wrist" appeared in *Hayden Ferry Review*

"Say You Say" appeared in *Heron Tree*

"Elegy for Snow & a Day that Did Not Belong to Her," "When the Body is a Guardrail," and "By Any Other Name" appeared in *Rising Phoenix*

"Under the Missing & Innumerable Stars" appeared in *Southword*

"Prayer for Winter," "A Thousand Lives Lived," and "Elegy for the River that Was" appeared in *Wordgathering*

"Everyone Knows Moonshine Tastes Better Illegal" and "Disappeared, TX" appeared in *The Sagebrush Review*

"Highway Elegy" appeared in *The New Poet*

"Country Life is Like the Negative Side" appeared in *Burnt District*

"Like Snow" and "Supernatural Scrabble" appeared in *Night Ride Home. Finishing Line Press*, 2012

And, as always, much love to my family for endless support, for those who stay even when disappearing is easier.

Kara **Dorris** is the author of *Have Ruin, Will Travel* (Finishing Line Press, 2019). She has also published five chapbooks: *Elective Affinities* (dancing girl press, 2011), *Night Ride Home* (Finishing Line Press, 2012), *Sonnets from Vada's Beauty Parlor & Chainsaw Repair* (dancing girl press, 2018), *Untitled Film Still Museum* (CW Books, 2019), and *Carnival Bound [or please unwrap me]* co-written with Gwendolyn Paradice (The Cupboard Pamphlet, 2020). Her poetry has appeared in *Prairie Schooner, DIAGRAM, I-70 Review, Rising Phoenix, Harpur Palate, Cutbank, Hayden Ferry Review, Tinderbox, Puerto del Sol, The Tulane Review,* and *Crazyhorse,* among others literary journals, as well as the anthology *Beauty is a Verb* (Cinco Puntos Press, 2011). Her prose has appeared in *Wordgathering, Breath and Shadow, Waxwing,* and the anthology *The Right Way to be Crippled and Naked* (Cinco Puntos Press, 2016). She earned a PhD in literature and poetry at the University of North Texas. Currently, she is a visiting assistant professor of English at Illinois College. For more information, please visit karadorris.com.

www.ingramcontent.com/pod-product-compliance
Lightning Source LLC
Chambersburg PA
CBHW021155090426
42740CB00008B/1094